1988

THE MISSIONS OF CALIFORNIA

Jan Breslauer for her invaluable

ublication Data

), 1948-
Stanley Young ; photography by

—California.   2. Spanish mission
al works.   3. California—
—Description and travel—1981-
                 II. Title.
                        88-12668
                        CIP

oast Books
er B.C. V5T 1C8

THE MISSIONS OF CALIFO

Photographs by

MELBA LEVICK

✣

Text by

STANLEY YOUNG

✣

Foreword by

SALLY B. WOODBRIDGE

Chronicle Books ✣ San Francisco

Chro
275 F
San Fr
94103

TABLE OF CONTENTS

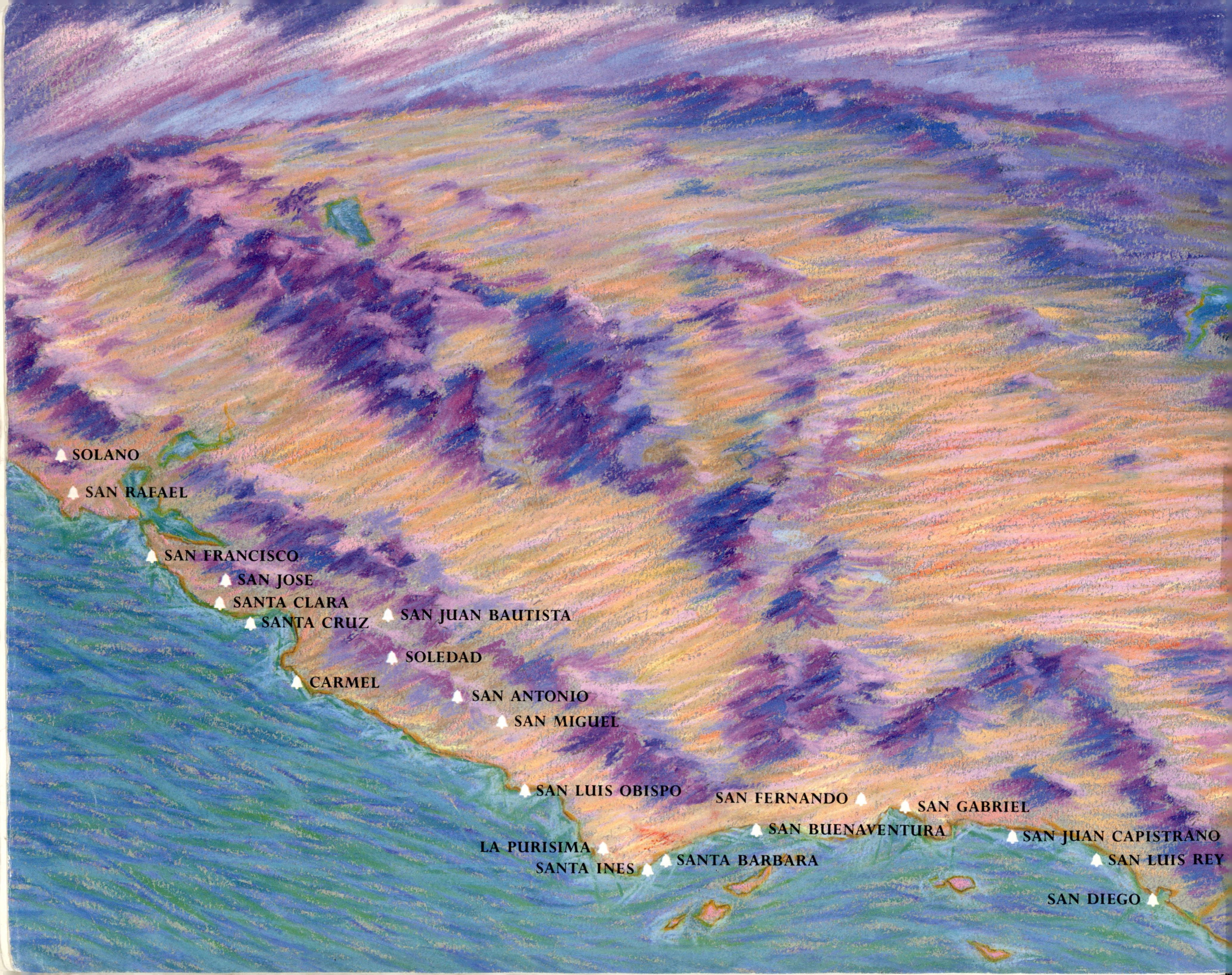

SOLANO

SAN RAFAEL

SAN FRANCISCO

SAN JOSE

SANTA CLARA

SANTA CRUZ

SAN JUAN BAUTISTA

SOLEDAD

CARMEL

SAN ANTONIO

SAN MIGUEL

SAN LUIS OBISPO

SAN FERNANDO

SAN GABRIEL

SAN BUENAVENTURA

SAN JUAN CAPISTRANO

LA PURISIMA

SAN LUIS REY

SANTA INES

SANTA BARBARA

SAN DIEGO

California and the Spanish Empire

When the first band of weary travelers reached San Diego in 1769 to found a mission—the first on that shore—the Spanish Empire was playing out its final act. It is surprising that Spain had waited so long to explore and settle this land, for Spanish explorers had discovered the California coast more than two centuries before. Juan Rodriguez Cabrillo had come here in 1542 and called the climate "*delicioso*"; Sebastian Vizcaino had sailed up the coast in 1602 and described a bay he named Monterey as "the best port that could be desired." Rumor had it that this "island" (as it was then thought to be) lay under the dominion of the beautiful Queen Califia, who ruled a nation of black-skinned Amazons.

With regard to their empire in the New World, however, the Spanish had been content to continue what they had established in Mexico and to exploit its known sources of silver and gold. They had firmed up their hold on Baja California and looked to the unknown north with a curious but unmotivated attitude. After all, getting there was difficult: land approaches were blocked by desert or mountains; sailing up the western coast of Baja was a constant battle against tireless headwinds. California, for all the rumors of riches that surrounded it, remained an undiscovered and remote land.

The Spanish attitude toward California changed when news reached Madrid that representatives of the czarina had crossed the Bering Strait and were establishing forts and outposts as far south as the Farallon Islands, not far from present-day San Francisco. With this Russian encroachment the Spanish determined, at last, to explore and settle Alta California; the order came from the king of Spain himself.

Elsewhere it was the Age of Reason, but not in the Spanish Empire. Locations, mountains and bays were named after martyrs, inquisitors and Crusaders; time itself was measured by saints' days and feast days. The Church was a predominant influence, and its monks embodied the crusading and medieval attitude toward the New World that had established Spain over half the globe. "All empire is power in trust," wrote John Dryden. The Spanish court had long before learned to entrust their power to the padres. Like others before them, many were driven and tireless men who had been assigned God's work, and no hardship, be it pestilence, hostile natives or famine, would stay the march to found missions—and secure the domain of the Spanish Empire.

In each instance a handful of soldiers armed with muskets and protected by thick leather jerkins backed up the padres' dogged devotion. This partnership of the sword and the cross had proved successful elsewhere in the Spanish Empire (especially South America) and served both equally; the Crown was interested in gold and trade while the padres were looking for souls.

From the point of view of the Spanish authorities, the missions, simply put, were cost effective. The padres received no pay, and their needs were few. Moreover, their role in the conversion of the local Indians was crucial to the plan of empire.

Few Spaniards were willing to colonize this newest land on the far ends of their empire. With no one available to follow the padres, they established colonies by a simple demographic maneuver; the plan was for the padres, through education, to transform the local Indians into civilized Spaniards—and thereby into the "colonists" of their own land.

To be sure, the padres were motivated by more than imperial efficiency. The Franciscans, who were given the task of founding the missions in Alta California, were devout followers of St. Francis of Assisi. Even amid the material bounty of the missions, once these small outposts had been turned into well-functioning enterprises, the padres never benefited personally from their labor. They were a devout group of men, who may have received their orders from kings and viceroys but ultimately looked to God for their authority.

Such a man was Junipero Serra. A native of the Balearic island of Majorca, he had been educated at the Lullian university in Palma, that island's capital. He held the Duns Scotus chair in philosophy at the same university for fifteen years before leaving for Mexico in 1749 at the age of thirty-seven to carry out his real calling: missionary work in the New World. After the king of Spain, wary of the Jesuits' growing political power, expelled the Society of Jesus from the Spanish Empire in 1767, the Franciscans were appointed to continue their work in Baja California, and Serra was chosen to lead them in that narrow peninsula. Two years later Jose de Galvez, the aide to the Spanish king's viceroy in Mexico, needed a strong-willed and determined cleric to head the founding of the first missions in Alta California. He turned to Serra.

Serra was a small man, not particularly robust, and he walked with a limp, the result of an injury sustained in his earliest days in Mexico. Nevertheless at the age of fifty-five he accepted the challenging task of founding a new chain of missions and set out, riding a mule most of the way, to cover the 750-mile journey to the first mission site at San Diego de Alcala, arriving in 1769. By the time of his death fifteen years later he had covered thousands more miles and founded nine other missions.

The man who succeeded him (following a brief, one-year term by Serra's biographer Francisco Palou) was cast in a mold similar to that of the founder of the first ten missions in California. Fermin Francisco de Lasuen was sixty-six when he assumed the office of president of the missions, and, like Serra, had been in Mexico since his thirties. During the eighteen years he presided over the mission chain, from 1785 to 1803, he founded eight missions and introduced the style of architecture—rounded roof tiles and wide arches—that is now commonly associated with the mission era.

We know a great deal about the missions and the men who founded and served in them thanks to the ever-present diarists who accompanied even the earliest and most dangerous expeditions. (The first book written in California was Palou's biography of Serra, written in 1785 in Carmel, now a valuable source of information about the founding of the first missions.)

Besides the work of the diarists, every mission kept meticulous records, showing the bookkeeping of both the material and spiritual sides of their enterprise: how many baptisms, how much wheat. These records and diaries provide an accurate picture of the golden age of the missions as seen through the eyes of a few hundred Spaniards and a few dozen padres.

The history from the point of view of the Indians was never recorded. Had their contemporary tale been written down, it would have constituted a painful list of tragedies involving not just hundreds but tens of thousands. Some Indians did benefit from the presence of the missions; most did not. At the time of the founding of the first mission there was an estimated population of some hundred thousand Indians in California. They lived in small, more or less sedentary nations and spoke a rich diversity of languages and dialects. Within the first decades of the coming of the white man to California, the majority of these Indians had died from diseases, such as measles, for which they had never developed an immunity.

Those Indians who survived helped fuel the material success of the padres' enterprise. Hundreds, sometimes up to a thousand converts would be involved with the running of a single mission. Each convert had a quota of labor to fulfill and, in return, received sacraments, food, clothing and education. Many Indians were taught the manual skills upon which the missions would thrive: animal husbandry, tallow making, hide and leather manufacture, adobe brick making, tile manufacture. The women were taught such skills as weaving and embroidery.

By entering into such arrangements with the mission, however, the converts gave up their previous lives forever. Once baptized and living next to the mission in their simple huts the converts, known to the Church as neophytes (literally the "newly planted"), belonged to the mission. If they attempted to flee, they were hunted down, and, if captured, brought back and punished. After the eventual secularization of all mission property the Indians no longer had the mission as the focus of their lives. Nor did they have their former tribal organization to return to, since in many cases the tribes had been wiped out by disease. From the Indian point of view, the introduction of the mission system meant cultural and physical genocide.

The historical irony is that the missionaries came with the purest of hearts and motives. They saw the local inhabitants as children, lost souls who needed the sacraments of God and the benefits of European civilization. In theory, each mission was a temporary institution that held all wealth and property in trust for the local Indians. Once the natives were appropriately civilized, the missions were to give up their stewardship of the land to create a pueblo for the Indians. (In theory, at least, this Spanish approach to the native people was more enlightened than that of the Protestant Americans, who simply drove the Indians off desired lands and forced them onto reservations.)

Given time, the orderly transfer of wealth from the Church to its followers might have happened. But secularization, which started as early as 1826 and continued well into the 1830's, took place in the turbulent period that followed the creation of the Mexican Republic. All Spanish-born padres were expelled, and Mexican settlers, who had legally been unable to own land, were enabled to buy it from the Indians. More often than not the settlers hoodwinked the new owners out of the land, or they simply took it. The orderly and lawful transition of property from Church to Indians broke down; the Indians lost everything. The land was subdivided and ended up in the great ranchos that were established at the time. Within a few short years the bulk of the missions' resources—land, crops, livestock—had been dispersed. Except for the rare mission such as Santa Barbara that continued to operate uninterrupted, and a few chapels that still functioned as parish churches, most of the missions were abandoned. In most cases all that survived were broken buildings, deserted fields and the names the padres had given them: San Diego, San Francisco, San Jose, Carmel. The names of saints, martyrs and apostles would remain to bear witness to the missions and the legacy they left the Golden State.

How the Missions Were Built

The founding of a mission was always celebrated with a mass, and the chapel or church (along with the stockade) was always the first building to be completed. Yet the actual house of worship was only part of a much larger complex, which in some cases spread over as much as six acres. Storehouses, workshops, soldiers'

barracks, mills and tanneries were just as essential to the missions.

In some cases, some of the larger missions were able to establish sub-missions, or *asistencias*. These outposts of the main missions often served a single purpose—as did San Rafael Arcangel, which, with its sun and warmth, was founded specifically as a sanitorium for converts in ill health. (Partly for reasons of empire San Rafael later became a full-fledged mission in its own right.) Of the six original *asistencias*, only one remains standing. San Antonio de Pala—situated twenty miles inland from its mother mission San Luis Rey de Francia—continues to serve the same Indian tribe for which it was originally established.

When it came to construction of the missions, the fathers had limited resources to work with. Many of the features of the missions that later entered the vernacular architecture of California were products of sheer necessity. Since the padres used readily produced adobe brick almost exclusively, the walls had to be thick and the arches squat simply to support their own weight. The long eaves and graceful overhangs later copied in houses and buildings served to protect the adobe walls from the elements. The rounded roof tiles served the same purpose.

The church was the centerpiece of each mission. The padres knew when they left Spain to serve God and carry the Word that they might never return. The churches they built show clearly the influence of their homeland; these buildings embody all the cultural complexity of Spain itself and, in addition, local Indian elements—especially in the colors of interior decoration.

The fathers would gladly have built cathedrals, had they had access to skilled labor. But given their resources they ended up with little more than large adobe structures. These simple churches were then embellished with allusions to the grandeur that they felt a building dedicated to God needed. Remove the facades and you are left with simple, crude and honest houses of God with low, pedestrian rooflines. Using adobe alone it was difficult for the padres to construct a four-sided bell tower. They chose, in most cases, to construct a single high wall with clean, arched spaces where the bells could hang. (The facades and the wall-style *campanarios* have since become the "trademark" of the missions.) The interiors are even more inventive. Lacking skilled stonecutters and masons, the fathers instructed local artists to *paint* the accoutrements of a cathedral: three-

MISSION SAN DIEGO

San Diego de Alcala

In Mission Valley, off Interstate 8. Daily 9–5.
619/281-8449.

The beginning of the California missions was by no means auspicious. The first expedition to establish Alta California consisted of four separate parties of Franciscans and soldiers— two by land and two by sea. Of the sea party, only 126 colonists of the original 226 survived the scurvy that struck as they battled continual headwinds up the coast of Baja California.

Don Gaspar de Portola, the newly appointed governor of Alta California, was in charge of the full expedition, composed of soldiers, Christian Indians from Baja California and a handful of Franciscans. One land party was headed by a Captain Rivera with the expedition's diarist, Father Juan Crespi; Portola himself led the other, accompanied by Serra, who had been assigned the task of supervising the establishment of all missions in the new territory by the Inspector-General Jose de Galvez, the King of Spain's personal representative in Mexico. On July 1, 1769, remnants of Portola's group, the last to reach the appointed spot on the coast, straggled in after a two-month journey through the arid and inhospitable Baja peninsula.

After a brief rest Portola and a small group of soldiers continued north to locate the supposedly magnificent Bay of Monterey, the site chosen by Galvez for the second mission to be established. Serra remained behind and wasted no time in establishing the mission complex, despite the many hardships and continuing losses the colonists were suffering. Within two weeks of his arrival a cross was erected on a rise overlooking the bay. (Today the site is known as Presidio Hill.) He chose to name the mission after a fifteenth-century Franciscan of lowly origins from Alcala who had been sainted in 1588. Five years later the mission was relocated to its present place in order to be nearer a fresh water supply and the residences of the local Indians.

The ceremony used to found San Diego became the prototype for the rites performed at all of the later missions. A large wooden cross was raised, mass was said, and the local Indians were summoned by bells hung from trees, then given trinkets to win their confidence. Though the gift-giving approach was often successful elsewhere, at San Diego the Indians resented the Spaniards' intrusion into their territory and attacked the crude settlement within the month. While their arrows flew through the air, Serra huddled in a brushwood hut praying that none of the Indians would be killed before being baptized. The father would have to wait a full year before the first such rite could be carried out on a single Indian child, but by the time a temporary church had been built, in 1774, relations with the indigenous peoples had improved and sixty Indians were baptized.

The native resistance continued, however, and the following year this first church structure was burned to the ground. During the attack an Indian arrow claimed the life of Father Luis Jayme, the first Christian martyr in California. His remains are now interred in the mission sanctuary. Following this bloody encounter the priests retreated to the presidio garrison where the soldiers were headquartered, and there they remained for two years. Eventually the Indians realized they couldn't compete with the Spanish guns, and they cooperated with the padres in rebuilding the church on the same charred grounds.

Also constructed in the first decade of the nineteenth century was a

large dam six miles upstream (parts of which are still visible). A large adobe church was dedicated in 1813. In its heyday the mission was a large complex of buildings surrounding a central square courtyard whose sides extended forty yards. After secularization the mission suffered badly, to the extent that for a period of twelve years it was used by the U.S. Army to stable horses. By the time restoration was begun, in 1931, all that remained of this "Mother of the Alta California Missions" was a ragged facade.

Today the simple church and its classic *campanario* share the great Mission Valley with tract condominiums and shopping centers. Hidden away against the hillside, this incongruous oasis remains in stubborn contrast to the football stadium only a short walk away. In 1976, Pope Paul VI deemed the present church a minor basilica (a church accorded certain ceremonial privileges), and today it continues as an active Catholic parish.

MISSION SAN LUIS REY

San Luis Rey de Francia

Five miles east of Oceanside on State Highway 76. Mon. through Sat. 10–4, Sun. 12–4; closed major holidays.
619/757-3651.

When Father Fermin Lasuen founded this mission in 1798 in a quiet inland valley, he chose to grace it with the name of the thirteenth-century king of France who left his country for the Holy Land to fight in the Crusades. As was so often the case with the missions, makeshift structures housed the worship services in the earliest years; in 1811, construction began on the present building. Father Antonio Peyri designed the original compound—completed four years later—and stayed on to manage the mission for more than thirty years. Under his conscientious administration the mission prospered and in a few years was able to support a branch mission, an *asistencia* (San Antonio de Pala), to serve the Indian tribes farther inland. (Today this *asistencia* is the only one of six such mission branches still standing.)

Peyri was among the most popular and versatile of the padres, and there are many stories of the veneration with which his Indian charges regarded him. One such tale surrounds his departure in 1829. After the Mexican expulsion decree that year Peyri stole away to San Diego without saying good-bye to the Indians of San Luis Rey. They pursued him the thirty miles to the port and caught up with him as he was about to board a ship bound for Spain. The Indians pleaded with him to return, but the Franciscan, forced to leave or suffer imprisonment, was able to offer them only a farewell benediction before the ship set sail. The Indian population of the mission never recovered from losing their beloved father. Following secularization the church lands were sold and the neophyte population dispersed.

Peyri is also remembered for the first pepper tree brought to California, although it was, in fact, planted a year after his untimely departure. Sailors had brought what they thought were chili pepper seeds from Peru in 1830; the plant that grew, however, turned out to be *schinus molle*, the rose-berried pepper tree with the filigreed foliage now an everyday sight throughout the state.

During the Mexican War San Luis Rey was used as a U.S. military outpost, and in 1893 the mission was redesignated a Franciscan college.

In its prime, San Luis Rey was one of the most extensive of all the missions, covering almost six acres. In addition to the religious buildings the complex also contained large soldiers' barracks, an elaborate sunken garden and a vast tiled laundry where Indian women washed clothes with water redirected from two local springs.

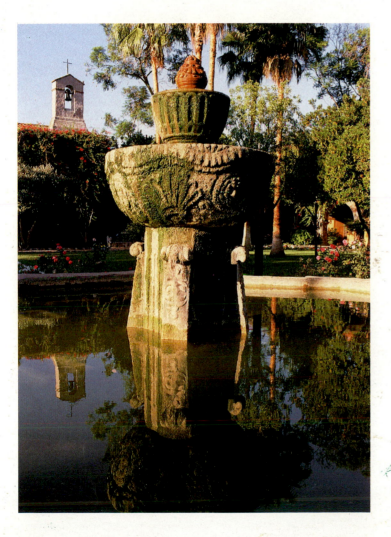

On Interstate 5, in the heart of the town of San Juan Capistrano, Daily 7:30–5. 714/493-1111.

The ever-vigorous Father Serra led an attempt to found this mission as early as 1775. No sooner had he and his fellows held initial ceremonies, however, than they received word of the violent Indian uprising at San Diego in which settlers had been attacked and one father killed. The newcomers feared that further hostility from the Indians could endanger Spanish occupation altogether, and they decided to forgo their new project for the moment.

It was not until a full year later that Fathers Lasuen and Serra returned to resume their work. Fortune, it seems, had not entirely abandoned them, for the cross they had erected at the original founding still stood to greet them upon their return, and the bells that had been stored away were stored still—and were retrieved and rung. The formal founding took place on November 1, 1776.

Within the year a simple adobe church was erected that still stands to this day. It is considered to be California's oldest building and is often referred to as "Father Serra's Church," for it is the only building where it is certain that the father-president said mass.

After two decades of increasing prosperity in the fertile setting, work began on an ambitious project to build a second church that would be a jewel among the missions. Indians of all ages hauled rocks from neighboring stream beds, and a skilled stonemason arrived from Culiacan,

Mexico, and stayed for nine years, the duration of the church's construction. The result was astonishing: the six domes of the vaulted roof stood 147 feet high; the foundation was 7 feet thick; the high bell tower could be seen from a distance of 10 miles and the peal of its bells could be heard from an even greater distance. Unfortunately the tabernacle stood for only a brief six years. During mass on December 8, 1812, the earth shook and the church collapsed, fatally trapping forty Indian worshipers under the rubble of the roof. Thereafter services were resumed in Father Serra's Church, and the mission continued for some fifteen years at its high level of material achievement before beginning a slow decline. By 1835, two years after the Mexican authorities freed the neophytes, there was little left to show of its former wealth, although the mission continued its enterprise in hides and tallow (as described in Richard Henry Dana's classic *Two Years before the Mast*).

Restoration in the 1890's saved Father Serra's Church from complete collapse, and further work in the 1920's, under the guidance of Father (later Monsignor) John O'Sullivan, created the mission more or less as it is now known.

The Franciscans' founder, St. Francis of Assisi, once called all birds his brothers. It is therefore fitting that the mission is today best known in popular lore for its famed swallows. Tradition has it that the birds take wing to fly south on the mission's namesake day, October 19, and return each spring on St. Joseph's Day, March 19.

While the Capistrano mission is beautiful under any conditions, it has a special quality at sunset when the remaining fragments of semi-Moorish architecture stand against the backdrop of nearby green hills and distant purple mountains. The walled garden secludes a taste of the Old World and the quiet of the original mission days. Swallows and mockingbirds flit and chirp among the olive trees and nearby walnut groves. In the fountain facing the ivy-covered ruins a flock of snow white doves flutters down to settle quietly for the night in what is, in fact, the "Jewel of the Missions."

MISSION SAN GABRIEL

San Gabriel Arcangel

At 537 W. Mission Dr., San Gabriel. Daily 9:30–4:15; closed major holidays. 818/282-5191.

The founding fathers were unfamiliar with their new land, and more than once they made the mistake of establishing a mission too near the banks of one of the beautiful but unpredictable California rivers. Such was the case in 1771 when they planted the first cross for the Mission San Gabriel on the edge of a river the soldiers had named Rio de los Temblores (River of the Earthquakes), now the San Gabriel River. Flash floods washed away their earliest crops of wheat and vegetables, and the fathers relocated to a site five miles north of the original location. This second choice, out of the river's range, was fortuitous, for it proved to be just as fertile and inviting as the first. Within a few years the new location was bustling with the activities of mission life, and by 1811 San Gabriel reaped the largest wheat crops ever recorded by the missions of Alta California. The mission stood in the heart of a veritable cornucopia.

Although in its time San Gabriel always played an important part as a crossroads of the major routes, this mission had to wait nearly half a century before being "discovered" by the Americans. Jedediah Smith was the first Yankee to see the mission, after he and his fellow trappers descended from the Sierras to San Gabriel in 1826. The weary overland trappers were accorded welcome hospitality by the fathers at the mission, and migrants that followed Smith looked to San Gabriel as an important way station

along their route into California. Here the hardy pioneers could replenish supplies after their difficult trek through the desert and mountains from Mexico through to Monterey.

The Spanish soldiers, and later the American adventurers who arrived at the doors of the mission, brought with them diseases for which the local indigenous peoples had little or no resistance. Most of the Indians fell victim to measles, small pox and venereal diseases; here, as elsewhere, the Indian population was devastated by such epidemics during the mission era.

Secularization in 1834 hit San Gabriel hard. The civilian administrator dismantled the mission holdings, and when the property reverted to the church, only nine years later, little was left of its former wealth. From 1859 to 1908 San Gabriel was administered as a parish church. At that point it was taken over by the Claretian Fathers, who fifteen years later turned it into their headquarters and a preparatory college.

The capped buttresses that give San Gabriel a decidedly Moorish feel are reminiscent of the cathedral in Cordova, birthplace of Father Antonio Cruzado, the padre placed in charge of building this structure. The Arab

influence is therefore not surprising, for that Spanish cathedral had itself once been a mosque. Some of the walls of this structure—104 feet long, 27 wide and 30 high—are estimated to be as much as 6 feet thick. The mission's massive proportions could not, however, withstand the 1987 earthquake, which left visible cracks in the roof and caused serious structural damage.

The San Gabriel graveyard, like those of other missions, holds the remains of thousands of Indians. A graveyard of a different kind—the bleak remains of what were extensive vineyards and orchards—also stands about the city of San Gabriel in testimony to a lost past.

MISSION SAN FERNANDO

San Fernando Rey de España

At 15151 San Fernando Mission Blvd., Mission Hills. Daily 9–4:30; closed major holidays.
818/361-0186.

Father Lasuen and his fellow padres had seemingly unlimited energy, driven by their faith in their mission to bring Christianity to the Indians of the new land. As just one example of Lasuen's ceaseless drive, witness Mission San Fernando Rey de España—the fourth mission he founded in a period of as many months.

The location presented problems from the start. The land that the fathers had set their sights on was already occupied by a settler named Francisco Reyes, then mayor of Pueblo Los Angeles. An amicable agreement was eventually reached, and records list Reyes as the godfather of the first infant baptized at San Fernando.

The mission was located in a prime location, along the principal highway leading to Los Angeles, making it a convenient stop for weary travelers. So popular a resting place was it that the fathers had to build additions onto the famous Long Building that served as the hostelry in order to accommodate the number of visitors who sought lodging. At its greatest, the mission's quadrangle was enormous—not far short of the length of a football field on a side—but all that remains today is the lengthy building that formed the western side of this enormous patio.

Following secularization of the missions, Andres Pico, brother of Gov. Pio Pico, leased several thousand acres of land that included the mission property. The governor then sold these lands to raise funds to fight off the

Americans. Juan Celis, the purchaser, later sold Andres Pico a half-interest, and the latter promptly made the mission his country home.

In 1851, U.S. Sen. McClay and his partners bought the northern half of the rancho, the southern half of which had previously been sold to Isaac Lankershim. These two purchases ended the mission era and began in earnest the development of the town of San Fernando, today one of the most expensive suburban locales in California.

In 1971 the Sylmar earthquake, 6.1 on the Richter scale, destroyed the small but fully restored chapel. Within three years it had been replaced by an exact replica.

41

Founder Of the Mission
Fermin Lasuen, O.F.M.

The Mexican uprising did much to destabilize the missions, and by 1836 San Buenaventura was caught in the middle of the fray. Two competing candidates for the local governorship battled at the mission, and the buildings bore scars from the bloody encounter for years afterward. This hardship was somewhat compensated for by the mission's relatively easy secularization, due in large part to the admirable administrative efforts of Rafael Gonzales. All of the land holdings were dispersed by 1845, and the church was not returned to church authority until 1862.

Victorian "improvements," particularly under Father Ciprian Rubio, included destroying interior decorations made by Indians, razing the sacristy and covering the original floor with one of wood. As he had done at San Luis Obispo and San Juan Bautista, Rubio hid the massive roof beams with his preferred covering of tongue-and-groove wood. Modern restoration completed in 1959, however, rectified most of the questionable architectural decisions.

This mission was once famous for its walled gardens, but today all that remains of that particular splendor is one lone palm. The seventh most productive in agriculture among the missions, San Buenaventura boasted many exotic fruits among its crops. A seven-mile-long aqueduct was part of the water system of this once richest of the missions, though the floods of 1866–67 all but destroyed the superstructure. Today the ruins of the aqueduct's massive foundations are the only mementoes of this mission's ambitious undertaking.

MISSION SANTA BARBARA

At 2201 Laguna St., Santa Barbara. Mon. through Sat. 9–5, Sun. 1–5; closed major holidays.
805/682-4713.

The red tile roofs of the tenth mission are nestled among palm trees just east of the city that also bears its name. With lush botanical gardens nearby and a scenic coastline a few minutes' drive away, Mission Santa Barbara is an inextricable and beautiful part of California's Spanish heritage.

Founded in 1786 and completed in 1820, the "Queen of the Missions" is best known for its unique architecture. The twin bell towers and the ornate Roman temple facade, built in this case by Chumash Indians, were inspired by the 27 B.C. renderings of Vitruvius Pollio. The Roman influence stems from the mission's namesake, a Christian Roman virgin beheaded by her pagan father for her faith. The irrigation system—perhaps the best engineered of any among the missions—and the active port in the nearby natural harbor also made Santa Barbara one of the busiest missions; it remains in use to this day. In fact, legend has it that the altar light has never been extinguished since the buildings were completed, more than a century and a half ago.

The legend may well be true. Despite secularization and the end of the mission era in 1830, Santa Barbara was never allowed to lapse into decay as were the other missions. It is also the only mission site that has remained continually under the authority of the Franciscans since its inception, a fact that may account for both its survival and continued preservation. The bishop's residence was moved here from San Diego in 1842, and eleven years later the mission was made a hospice and apostolic college for the schooling of novitiates. Between 1868 and 1877 a Franciscan boys' school flourished on the site, and shortly before the turn of the century (1896) a seminary was established. The Franciscan School of Theology was housed at Santa Barbara until 1968.

Today, the Franciscans still minister to Indians of the Southwest, and the church itself houses the parish of St. Barbara. Here, too, you can visit a museum of the mission era and the archives of the Franciscan order, which include a large collection on Junipero Serra and all the important state documents dating from before the American takeover.

The mission graveyard probably looks much as it did a century ago.

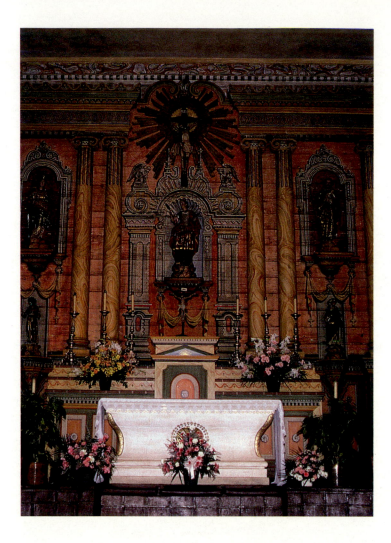

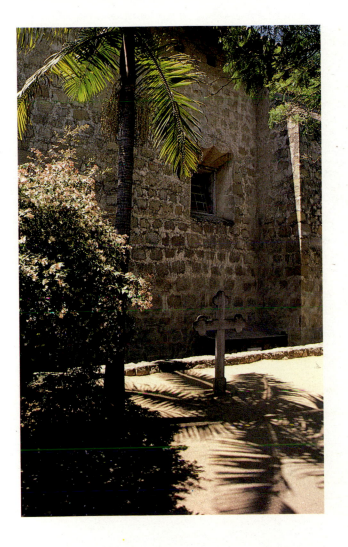

Surrounded by high adobe walls and shaded by trees, their limbs bent with age, it is the resting place of more than four thousand Indians, many of them victims of diseases brought by the white man for which they had no natural resistance. Here also lie the remains of Juana Maria, "the wild woman of San Nicolas Island." In 1835 a ship sent by the padres arrived at San Nicolas Island to remove the few remaining Indians and bring them to live at the mission, where new workers were needed. On the return journey one of them, Juana Maria, jumped overboard and swam back to her only child, who had been left behind. The sailors let her go and she was soon forgotten and assumed drowned. Almost two decades later a fisherman found her, on the island still, now a thin wisp of a woman dressed in woven feathers. She was brought to the mission, but she died shortly afterward. A plaque with her name engraved was installed by the Daughters of the American Revolution in 1928 and is one of the few monuments in the mission chain commemorating an individual Indian.

MISSION SANTA INES

At 1760 Mission Dr., Solvang, 3 miles east of Buellton off Route 246. Mon. through Sat. 9:30–4:30 (except June through Aug. 9–5), Sun. 12–4:30; closed major holidays.
805/688-4815.

Purple mountains in the distance dwarf the humble mission that rises from fields in the valley of Calahuasa, a day's travel from Mission Santa Barbara, thirty miles to the southeast. From the small graveyard it is possible to see nearby Solvang, a town founded by Danish farmers in the nineteenth century. The modest original chapel was destroyed in the quake of 1812, and a brick and adobe building was completed in 1817 that stands to this day.

Father Estevan Tapis, who succeeded Father Lasuen after Lasuen's death in 1803, is credited with originally spotting this site the following year. As with its sister inland churches the Mission Santa Ines was established to minister to the many Indians who lived scattered about the coast range. Estimates place the local population at the time at around eleven hundred, a sizable population for the fathers to convert and a challenge they gladly accepted.

By the time the fathers arrived the Indians had already heard of the missionary crusades; some two hundred eagerly awaited the blessings that the fathers gave as soon as the altar was set down. That first day twenty children were baptized.

Despite the auspicious beginning Santa Ines was the scene of one of the largest recorded Indian uprisings only twenty years later. Spanish soldiers stationed at the missions were often an illiterate and sadistic lot. At

This mission is named in honor of a thirteen-year-old martyr, Agnes, who was executed in 304 A.D. in Rome for her refusal to make a pagan sacrifice. She died a lonely death for her faith. The mission that bore her name in Spanish had a life span of only thirty-two years, and, isolated and removed from most of the thoroughfares, was among the loneliest assignments a padre could be given. Visitors were so infrequent that when one was spotted the mission bells were rung to announce the event, summoning padres and neophytes throughout the lonely valley to come and greet the approaching travelers at the main door.

Madonna Chapel
Center piece above
the Altar is a 17 CV.
polychromed wood
carving of the
Mother of Sorrows
La Soledad
Crucifix overhead is a
polychromed 18 C4.
Mexican woodcarving.
PLEASE DO NOT STEP
BEYOND THIS POINT.

MISSION LA PURISIMA

La Purisima Concepcion

Four miles northeast of Lompoc, 14 miles west of Buellton, via State Highway 246. Daily 9–4:30; closed major holidays.
805/733-3713.

Surrounded by trees and bare scrub La Purisima stands alone and proud in its hilly landscape a few miles from Lompoc. The original La Purisima, however, was less than one mile south of Lompoc's town center, a site chosen by Father Lasuen, who founded this once-prosperous mission in 1787. Perhaps because the town was so small the Church made an exception to its practice of placing missions no closer than seven miles from any city center.

The first, temporary building, erected in 1788, was replaced by an adobe and tile structure that was completed in 1802. With no adjacent port, and in light of its small surrounding population, the mission was never considered a vital outpost and was left to deteriorate. The earthquake of 1812 demolished the modest mission, leaving behind only a few partial walls. (A gash in the hillside just behind the ruins reminds visitors today of the force of the quake.) A new building was constructed east of what is now Lompoc, but the Indian uprising of 1824 took a heavy toll on both converts and clergy. These facilities also suffered considerable damage, and La Purisima slid once again into increasing disrepair.

Eventually, after this series of natural and historical disasters, La Purisima fell victim to both its neglect and the ravages of the elements. It lay in ruins for many years, the few lonely archways and elegant white pillars a silent testimony to its former stature. In the 1930's the state of California

acquired the mission and began an energetic and thorough process of restoration.

La Purisima is presently distinguished as the most fully restored—one might almost say wholly rebuilt—of all the missions. The state took great pains to reproduce the mission in its entirety, down to the gardens now filled with typical herbs, fruits and vegetables of the era. A solitary stone settling tank in a nearby canyon is one of the few authentic traces of the earliest days of the Franciscans in this harsh setting.

DO NOT
PICK GRAPES
PLEASE

MISSION SAN LUIS OBISPO

San Luis Obispo de Tolosa

In the town of San Luis Obispo, at the corner of Monterey and Chorro streets.
Mon. through Sat. 9–4, Sun. 8:30–5; closed major holidays.
805/543-1034.

Even after three fires had ravaged this outpost of the Church in the decade since its founding by Serra in 1772, none of the fathers was willing to abandon it. Instead, the misfortunes guided them to new strengths, and under the leadership of Father Jose Cavaller they sought to replace the combustible thatched roofs with something more resilient and less flammable.

The fathers determinedly set about to manufacture tile in California. Draft animals were used to wedge the local wet clay with their hooves, and the clay was allowed to sit, then applied to the surface of smooth, hemicylindrical forms. The sun-dried "green" tiles were then fired in a wood-burning kiln. The first attempts were so successful and practical that by 1784 all the missions had adopted this new method of roofing. Henceforth the sight of the rounded, red roof tiles would be synonymous with the Spanish missions, and the padres' innovation at San Luis Obispo would leave an indelible mark on California and Californian architecture.

Though the usual practice was to station two padres at each mission, Father Cavaller served his tenure there all alone until his death in 1789. His replacement, Father Luis Martinez, was famous for a portly physique and brusque manner. This padre's legendary sense of the droll is well illustrated by the story of the "poultry parade" he organized when faced with the need to entertain guests General Moreno and his new bride. As related in Helen H. Jackson's novel *Ramona*, Indians herded all the birds belonging to the mission through the corridors for nearly an hour while the general and his bride laughed with abandon. The outspoken Father Martinez was less appreciated by some officials of the government, however, and he was forced to leave the country in 1830, banished by the governor on a trumped-up charge after thirty-four years of service at the mission.

After secularization the mission lay neglected until it was transformed, in 1875, into the center of a bustling little town, complete with an ornate French Hotel. At that point, however, the rugged little church was encumbered by unenlightened attempts at restoration. The roof tiles were removed, an incongruous New England bell steeple was added, and the facade was covered with wooden clapboard. Inside, tongue-and-groove boards were used to cover the roof and wooden boards to disguise the stone and mortar (*mezcla*) floor. Ironically, a fire exposed the true soul of the building, in 1920. The charred false wooden ceiling was removed, revealing the original hand-hewn beams that supported the roof. The white wooden external siding, however, was not removed until 1934. The mission church is now the active parish of San Luis Obispo, the city that grew up about the small mission in La Cañada de los Osos—the Valley of the Bears.

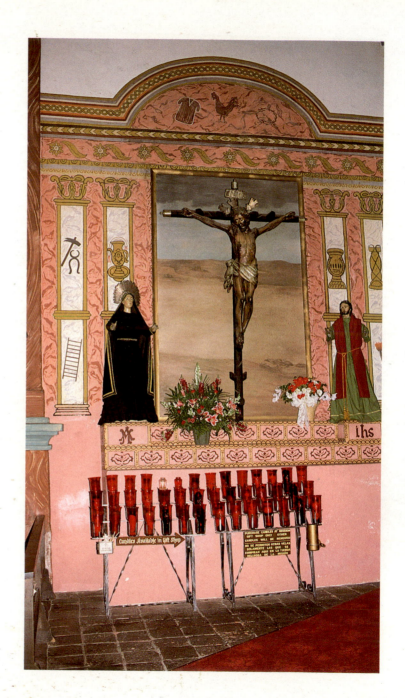

MISSION SAN MIGUEL

San Miguel Arcangel

Eight miles north of Paso Robles, off U.S. Highway 101. Daily 9:30–4:30 (except June through Aug. 9–5).
805/467-3256.

Father Fermin Lasuen and Father Buenaventura Sitjar located the Mission San Miguel Arcangel in 1797 in a lush nook of the Salinas River. They chose the serene location not only for its beauty but, as with other inland outposts, to cater to the large population of potential converts. Additionally they were convinced there would be an abundant supply of water for agriculture, a key factor in the creation of a prosperous mission. The fathers' original optimism was well placed. At the height of their productivity, the mission lands extended more than fifty miles from end to end; the remains of the extensive network of dams and viaducts built by the fathers for irrigating their orchards may still be seen.

The Indians were at first excited and enthusiastic about the presence of the padres, as is evidenced by the fifteen baptisms on founding day and the subsequent one thousand converts over the next four years. After Jose Echeandia, the governor sent from Mexico, issued a declaration of independence for those Indians who wished it in 1831, Jose Castro, the new local commissioner, personally announced this decree at the mission. Through an interpreter he asked all those Indians wishing freedom from the demanding attachments to the mission to stand on his left; those who wished to remain with the father were to step to the right. Surprisingly, as the tale goes, not a single convert opted for secular freedom. Eight years later, however, the neophyte population was down to two hundred, and the herds and stocks had fallen accordingly.

This mission was accorded the mixed blessing of restoration considerably later and to a lesser extent than most of the other missions. As a result, you can still view original decor and handiwork. The rafters and corbels, for example, were hewn from trees by the Indians after they had transported the wood from the nearest mountains, forty miles away. Estevan Munras, a professional artist, supervised the Indians in decorating the church's interior, and much of their original artwork survives unretouched. San Miguel also has a variety of arch shapes and sizes in its colonnade, a characteristic unique among the existing mission structures.

ORIGINAL MISSION BELL
CAST IN MEXICO IN 1795
BY RUELAS FAMED MEXICAN
BELL-MAKER

MISSION SOLEDAD

Nuestra Señora de la Soledad

On Fort Romil Rd., 3 miles southwest of Soledad. Daily except Tuesday 10–4. 408/678-2586.

Thirty miles south of Monterey and one mile west of the Salinas River the land appears limitless, with fields and plains stretching for miles in every direction. It was here, in 1791, at the beginning of the golden age of the California missions, that Father Lasuen planted the cross and rang the bells heralding the founding of Mission Soledad. The idyllic yet isolated location has changed little since then, remaining a peaceful outpost to this day.

The mission lands were beautiful and spacious but never proved as well suited for pasturage or cultivation as the father had hoped. In its earliest years, growth was slow. Gradually, however, this peaceful mission flourished and became prosperous, although it was never as celebrated and well visited as some of the more accessible coastal missions along the Camino Real, the Royal Road that linked the mission chain. When the pirate Hippolyte de Bouchard began his raids on the coastal missions in 1818, many clergy and civil governors took refuge in Soledad, the most isolated outpost of the mission chain.

So desolate was an assignment at Soledad that thirty padres served there in the forty-four years it was in operation. When Father Vicente Sarria perished there in 1835 a few of his loyal converts carried his emaciated body to San Antonio de Padua and left Mission Soledad forever to its demise. It then, like most other missions, lapsed into the cycle of abuse, disrepair and finally ruin.

In 1952 a group of women throughout the state known as the Native Daughters of the Golden West undertook the rebuilding of the small mission. Once it was restored the maintenance of the site and buildings was handed over to a committee of local citizens.

The modest building of this solitary mission stands in the shadows of haystacks and nearby pastured cattle, the land about it vast and dry. Its fate reinforces how aptly it was named, for the Virgin, "Our Lady of Solitude," whose effigy now stands over the altar, starkly dressed in the black garb of a Spanish widow.

MISSION CARMEL

San Carlos Borromeo de Carmelo

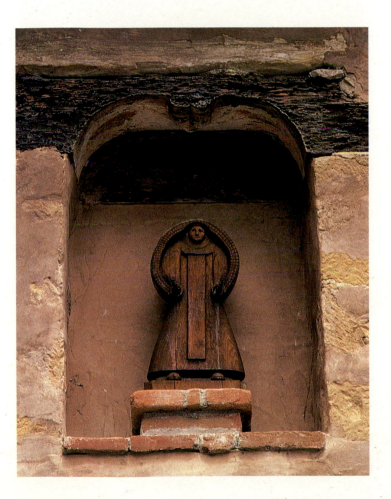

In Carmel, 3080 Rio Rd. Mon. through Sat. 9:30—4:30; Sun. 10:30—4:30; closed Christmas Day.
408/264-1271.

For the missionaries in Alta California getting the answer to a simple request from headquarters could take months from Mexico or, if the problem required an answer from Spain, well over a year. Those who set out to found the missions, therefore, planned everything well in advance, striking out for the new lands with long lists of instructions for every possible occasion. In the earliest days, however, not everything went according to these meticulous preparations.

In the original plan for the colonization of California, Monterey was to be the northernmost mission site, a decision designed in part to stem the Russians' descent along the Pacific coast. The choice for this outpost was based on a glowing description of the harbor by the Spanish explorer Vizcaino written more than a century and a half before. He had written that "we found ourselves to be in the best port that could be desired. . . ." In 1769 Portola looked in vain for such a bay; he planted a cross in a large bay that offered scant protection from the storm winds of the Pacific and continued in his search for what Vizcaino had described. On Portola's desperate return the following year he realized that he had been right all along. Vizcaino's exaggerated description had deceived him, and the cross Portola had planted did in fact overlook Monterey Bay.

Shortly thereafter, Father Serra arrived and Mission San Carlos Borcia Mountains, was designed by master mason Manuel Ruiz and completed in 1797. The scenic and fertile location within view of the vast Pacific made this mission a favorite of the hierarchy, and it became the headquarters for each father-president until that honor was transferred to Santa Barbara, shortly after Lasuen's death, in 1803.

After secularization Carmel passed through decades of neglect and collapse; the roof timbers shattered under the weight of the tiles, and for thirty years the church stood without cover. In 1882 Father Angelo Casanova opened the tombs in the sanctuary before an audience of more than four hundred, to quell rumors that Serra's remains had been removed.

MISSION SAN JUAN BAUTISTA

On the town square in San Juan Bautista, off State Highway 156. Daily Mar. 1 through Oct. 31, 9:30–5, and Nov. 1 through Feb. 28, 9:30–4:30; closed major holidays.
408/623-2127.

The hierarchy might have perhaps been wiser to name this fifteenth mission after San Andreas, for Father Lasuen chose as its site a golden plain in the center of the expansive San Benito Valley that stood directly over the infamous fault that came to bear Saint Andrew's name.

The mission, founded in 1797, was graced with the name of John the Baptist, however. Though the first building had only a mud roof, a permanent church followed; its cornerstone was laid in 1808. Encased inside this first, brick segment was a bottle containing an account of the founding festivities.

The altar and altarpiece (*reredos*) were painted ten years later by Bostonian Thomas Doak, a deserter from the ship *Albatross* who later married the daughter of a local grandee and became the first American settler in Alta California. Doak undertook the "commission" in trade for room and board after the local Mexican artist demanded the exorbitant sum of six reales (seventy-five cents) a day.

Father Estevan Tapis retired to San Juan Bautista in 1812, after completing a six-year term as father-president of the mission chain. He was an especially gifted music director, and the boys' choir at the mission was recognized as among the best in the territory, due perhaps to the meticulously prepared music parchments that the father devised for the young singers. Tapis was buried in the sanctuary upon his death at age seventy-one.

Father Felipe del Arroyo de la Cuesta, another of the missionaries of San Juan Bautista and a renowned linguistic scholar, was able to give his sermons in seven San Juan Indian dialects. In 1815, seven years after his arrival, he published one of a handful of studies of California Indian languages—in his case an overview of the Mutsun language. (Almost half a

century later, the Smithsonian Institution would publish an edited version of this early linguistic tract.) At the mission he was known as a gentle man, especially fond of children, whom he named—as the classical scholar he was—according to his literary heroes of antiquity. The various Platos and Ciceros would sing and dance to entertain this benevolent padre when he tired of his scholarly pursuits.

The mission was restored in 1884. After the 1906 earthquake that ravaged San Francisco, concrete buttresses were built to support the damaged walls, which, at forty feet in height, were the tallest adobe structures in any mission in the chain. Extensive repairs of the damage done by that disaster were not carried out until 1976. Only one of the original nine bells is still there, though the *campanario* has been completely rebuilt. Surprisingly, the nave chapel has survived intact, complete with the arch corridors that traverse the entire length of the building.

The cemetery wall now overlooks one of the rare remaining sections of the original Camino Real—the north-south highway that joined all the missions, and which largely became today's U.S. 101. The mission itself now fronts a plaza on which there's a restored version of the old village, including a hotel, stable and two adobe houses. Visitors can get an idea of what the community looked like before the Gold Rush days thanks to the restoration of the original buildings by the state of California in 1933.

MISSION SANTA CRUZ

At Emmet and High streets in Santa Cruz. Daily, 9–5. 408/426-5686.

When Portola and his band of explorers passed through the area where the twelfth mission would stand, they were all astounded at the monstrous trees that surrounded them. Father Crespi, the chronicler of the expedition, thought they were akin to cedars and named the trees, some of which rose into the air 350 feet, *palo colorado*. The Spanish had discovered the redwood, later to be designated America's national tree.

Members of a later expedition, in 1774, suggested the area as a pueblo and mission site. Although the region was inviting in every respect the cross for Mission Santa Cruz was not raised until August 28—San Agustin Day—1791. The original location, hard by the ocean at the end of the San Lorenzo Valley, was found to be too close to the water, and the church was moved to higher ground on the nearby mesa overlooking lush vegetation and the San Lorenzo River. From the bluffs to the west one can see the Pacific Ocean.

Adjacent Branciforte (named after the then viceroy, the Spanish king's personal representative in Mexico) was California's first planned community. It was arranged along the lines of a Roman colony, with the buildings centering on a plaza. Although it was ostensibly illegal to place a town within seven miles of a mission, and despite the padres' continual opposition, the governor upheld the town's founding by a private developer named Diego de Borica. A surprisingly modern promotion scheme enticed new settlers to the area, though they arrived to find, contrary to promises made, that no houses had been constructed for them. The padres and Borica were equally disappointed with the character of the new "pioneers"—particularly their propensity for gambling and thievery.

Many adventurers, native and foreign, were attracted to the new community, which proved to be the downfall of the mission; the population of Santa Cruz never rose much above five hundred, the lowest recorded for any mission in the chain. Elsewhere it was the indigenous people who attacked the missions, but at Santa Cruz the padres had to contend with their own unsavory countrymen.

When the pirate Hippolyte de Bouchard appeared offshore in 1818 the worst was feared. He had already attacked and ravaged the presidio at Monterey, and Governor Pablo de Sola ordered the resident padre, Father Olbez, to seek immediate refuge at the Santa Clara mission. Indians under Spanish command were dispatched to Santa Cruz to save what they could of the mission's goods and defend the property against the seafaring brig and Bouchard. The local populace was ordered to help in moving the church's property inland.

Had Bouchard reached the mission he might have dealt with it less severely than did the local Brancifortians. These settlers were only too happy to oblige the governor's decree and helped themselves to the bulk of what they could carry and were supposed to be saving. Then, emboldened by drink, the rabble looted the mission, soiled the vestments and defaced the images. Father Olbez was distraught upon his return, and requested permission to leave the mission. His request was denied.

An 1840 earthquake caused extensive damage, and the buildings were toppled for good in 1857. A frame church and then a brick church were constructed on parts of the original site. A granite arch was raised to signify hopes for more permanent construction in front of the brick church

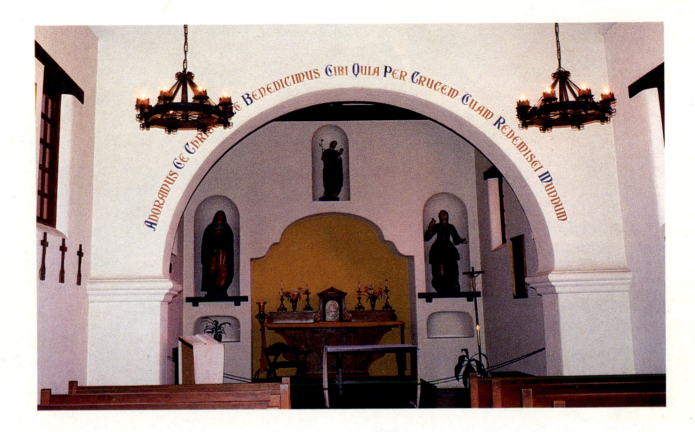

in 1891, a full one hundred years after the founding of Santa Cruz.

A one-third-size replica of the original mission was finished in 1931. Many of the artifacts of the first mission are housed here, including a number of vestments worn by the padres. A few trees and several tombstones from the original orchards and small graveyard also remain. Church records indicate that in 1835 Santa Cruz possessed ten mission bells, valued at $3,500—the highest value for any in the mission chain. Their whereabouts remain a mystery to this day.

a charter was issued in 1855 it was not until 1912 that Santa Clara attained the rank of university.

The present complex is a mix of new and restored buildings, including a few relics of the past. A concrete structure simulating the original adobe church was finished in 1928, and many artifacts of the earliest days are preserved within its walls. Olive trees planted by the first padres still shade the remaining adobe walls of the first cloisters. Here in this garden survives more of the original flora than at any other mission. An original Castilian rosebush, the oldest grapevine in northern California, and three "fan" palms (also known as Washingtonia palms, the only variety native to the state) date back to 1822. These mementoes from the mission era are eloquent testimony to the heritage of the Spanish that lives on in California to this day.

MISSION SAN JOSE

San Jose de Guadalupe

In Fremont at the junction of Highway 238 and Washington Blvd. Daily 10–5. 415/657-1797.

The ever-vigilant Father Lasuen hadn't anticipated the attitude of his neighboring Indians when he decided in 1797 to dedicate this mission on a site some fifteen miles north of the pueblo of the same name. Many of the indigenous nations bitterly resented the instrusion of the missionaries, and even those who were more accommodating were often little more than indifferent to what the padres had to offer.

Problems with the Indians were exacerbated by the strategic location of this mission at the head of the San Joaquin Valley. Indians who engaged in skirmishes with the Spanish leather-jackets on a regular basis lived in the vicinity, and they often gave refuge to fugitive neophytes. At least one infamous conflict broke out when Sgt. Pedro Amador waged a battle to bring back the runaways. Reprisals and further battles between the Indians and the Spanish followed sporadically.

Nonetheless, the mission flourished, and Father Narciso Duran, during his twenty-seven-year tenure here, created an acclaimed Indian orchestra, complete with contrabass and uniforms for the members. Certainly one of the more interesting characters to people the missions, this unusual padre also was a military strategist and served three terms as father-president of the mission chain.

A simulation of the original buildings was completed between 1982 and 1985, and today the mission and its decor probably look much as they did during the 1830s, when San Jose de Guadalupe was at its glory prior to secularization.

MISSION DOLORES

San Francisco de Asis

At 16th and Dolores streets, San Francisco. Daily 9–4; closed major holidays. 415/621-8203.

San Francisco de Asis is the third most northern mission, and the sixth to be begun under the auspices of Father Junipero Serra. Unlike most other missions, which were known by simply shortening their appellations to the saints' first names only (Santa Clara, San Diego), San Francisco de Asis came to be known by the nickname Mission Dolores. The mission's affectionate name came from that of a small nearby stream that no longer exists, Arroyo de Nuestra Señora de los Dolores. ("Dolores" means "sorrows.") The name probably had more ironic roots, however, for a posting to Mission Dolores meant enduring long periods of fog and damp—cold, unhealthy weather.

Surprisingly, the mission's official name and that of the Bay it graced were established before the Spanish even knew the Bay's exact location. The story is told that Serra asked *Visitador-General* Don Jose de Galvez "Is there to be no mission for our Father St. Francis?" to which he received the curt reply, "If St. Francis desires a mission let him cause his port to be discovered."

Although the Bahia de San Francisco had first been discovered—and named—by a Spanish explorer in 1597, the Bay remained overlooked in ensuing years because of its narrow entrance. Even when Portola stumbled through the Golden Gate while searching for the Monterey harbor in 1760 he thought the expanse of water to be an arm of the sea, and not

117

a bay at all. When, at last, the importance of the Bay to this northernmost region of the Spanish Empire was established, the Spanish viceroy ordered not one but two missions to be established, one—San Francisco—with a presidio to protect the entrance to the enormous Bay, and Serra's question was answered. (Santa Clara, founded one-half year after San Francisco de Asis, was the second mission to protect the Bay.)

The first, rudimentary church was established five days before the American Declaration of Independence in Philadelphia. The present church was begun in 1782 and finished by 1791. In contrast to the other missions it is strikingly simple in style, with neither the usual arches and arcades nor the typical detail. Instead it is distinguished by a massive facade and overall clean lines unusual in church architecture during the era of its founding.

The ancient adobe structure survived secularization and also the 1906 earthquake. Despite its age, the unpretentious chapel is still in good condition, and it is perhaps the least restored of all the churches in the mission chain. The original bells, all cast within five years of the church's completion in 1791, are still rung during Holy Week.

The occupants of the cemetery alongside the structure include both the famous and the anonymous. Don Luis Antonio Arguello, the first governor of Alta California under Mexican authority (from 1822 to 1825), and Don Francisco de Haro, San Francisco's first mayor, both rest here. When the grounds, which were originally much more extensive, were reduced, the unidentified remains of other deceased were laid in a common grave. The Grotto of Our Lady of Lourdes shrine marks the place of these forgotten dead.

MISSION SAN RAFAEL ARCANGEL

San Rafael Arcangel

In San Rafael, at the corner of Fifth Ave. and Court St. Mon. through Sat. 11–4, Sun. 10–4; closed major holidays. 415/456-3016.

On the return of Spanish Lt. Gabriel Moraga from a diplomatic mission to the Russians at Fort Ross, in 1816, he journeyed through the land of the Tamal Indians and happened upon a delightful spot known to the indigenous people as Nanaguani. He seized on the spot as a prudent site for a settlement that would establish Spanish domain on land north of San Francisco Bay and preempt the encroachment of the Russians, who were only a three-day ride to the north. It was, as well, a particularly salubrious location: the weather there was warm and clear and the views were impressive; Mount Tamalpais and rolling hills stretched off to the south and a large rise (later to be called San Rafael Hill) protected the site from the rear. Lieutenant Moraga convinced the padre at San Francisco to allow some of the ill converts there to leave Mission Dolores, with its cold, fog and damp, and spend some time at Nanaguani with its balmy weather and healthful air.

The ailing Indians (many of whom were suffering from "white man's diseases") arrived at the chosen spot and quickly recuperated, so the padres went on to establish there an *asistencia*, a sub-mission, that would serve the larger Mission Dolores primarily as a sanatorium. The following year, 1817, a cross was planted and the mass said to found the mission called after the angel whose name—Rafael—translates from the original Hebrew as "Healer of God." Father Luis Gil y Taboada, proficient both in the local idioms and basic medicine, began construction of the simple adobe building, eighty-seven feet long by forty-two wide, that would house the chapel and living areas for the new mission/sanatorium. The founding padre was a wise choice, and within the year the population of San Rafael was up to three hundred. By 1822 the *asistencia*, then under the leadership of Father Juan Amoros, was raised to full mission status.

Within a few years only a small portion of the mission population was converts in ill health from Mission Dolores. Under Amoros' industrious guidance San Rafael began to resemble its sister missions to the south, with a population that hovered around a thousand and an ample production of livestock, grains, vines and fruit.

The mission had a short life span, however; San Rafael was the first of all the mission chain to be secularized, in 1833. The rapacious Gen. Mariano Vallejo took all of the mission's property—and, when the mission Indians were unable to manage the physical plant themselves, he distributed these converts throughout his own ranchos, to work for mere subsistence. The mission buildings deteriorated rapidly, although Capt. John Fremont still found the buildings habitable when he lodged there with his forces during the Mexican War, early in the summer of 1846. Some years later the original buildings were razed and a new parish church was built on the site. The present replica, built on the approximate site of the original hospital mission, was completed in 1949. There were no drawings of the interior, and only a few old paintings of the mission's exterior. The simple star window that was built in the wall over the plain doorway was originally copied from the mission at Carmel; it is one of the few architectural details of which historians are certain.

MISSION SOLANO

San Francisco de Solano

In Sonoma off the plaza. Daily 10–5; closed major holidays. 707/938-1519.

This mission, the last in the chain to be built, had its inception in political subterfuge. Father Jose Altimira, the last of the padres to be born in Spain, arrived in 1819 in Alta California and was immediately seized with the pioneering spirit. His dream was to establish a mission on the northernmost edge of the Spanish Empire, amid the heathen, there to defend Spain against the southernly expanding Russian presence.

Altimira turned to the new Governor Arguello with a daring proposal: suppress Mission Dolores (San Francisco) and its offspring San Rafael and build a glorious new mission, a new San Francisco, farther to the north. On the tenth day after landing near San Rafael, Altimira chose a site about twenty miles north, close to a spring that rose near a hillside. His plan to have the two more southern missions closed was quashed as soon as it was discovered by his fellows, but he was allowed to continue the establishment of his new effort, named after a missionary to Peruvian Indians.

Altimira received little support from the other missions—only Mission Dolores sent livestock—but surprisingly the Russians sent vases, missal stands, linens, silks and even a bell from their outpost at Fort Ross. Altimira called the area surrounding his chosen site "The Valley of the Moon," after an observation the indigenous peoples had made concerning the moon in winter, when it would appear seven times in succession from behind distant mountain peaks. The valley's enticing name would later be used by Jack London as the title of a book, after the writer moved to nearby Glen Ellen.

In the years following the mission's establishment Altimira built up its physical plant. Provision of a long adobe building, 120 feet by 30, plus a chapel and several smaller buildings for a granary, was soon matched by the prolific output of newly planted wheat and barley fields, vines and orchards.

Altimira was infamous for his temper and his floggings, and in 1826 disgruntled Indians attacked and sacked the mission. The padre was lucky to escape with his life. He was replaced by Father Buenaventura Fortuni, who attempted to reconstruct the buildings but whose tenure was brief.

In 1834 the mission was secularized, and its land and convert-workers were dispersed.

Governor Vallejo built the town of Sonoma around the mission complex. The mission buildings received a modicum of upkeep, but without a missionary they were soon turned to more profitable uses; for several years, until their collapse, some mission structures were used for storing hay and making the local wine. In 1841 a simple chapel, now standing, was built alongside the original mission quadrangle.

This new chapel also quickly fell into disrepair. The site was purchased in 1903 by the California Historic Landmarks League, which repaired the building in 1911 with the help of the state. Further renovations and reconstruction took place in 1943–44, and the mission now stands as part of the Sonoma Mission State Historic Park.

INDEX

Editing   CAREY CHARLESWORTH

Book and cover design   HERMAN + COMPANY

Composition   WILSTED & TAYLOR

Map illustration   MICHÈLE MANNING